Dented Crown

Michelle R. Bostic

ISBN 978-1-68517-838-3 (paperback)
ISBN 978-1-68517-839-0 (digital)

Christian Faith Publishing
832 Park Avenue
Meadville, PA 16335
www.christianfaithpublishing.com

Definitions from Google
Bible scriptures found in the NIV version

Printed in the United States of America

Preface

I literally have two children; figuratively, I had three. God impregnated me several years ago with this book.

My first child is Mica. I dreamed of her before I knew I was pregnant, and in this dream, I was asleep as I would do in real life on my days off. She came to the side of the bed, when she was about three years old, and she said, "Wake up, Mommy. Play with me."

I said, "Not now, Mica. Mommy is sleeping."

I woke up the next day and told her dad I was pregnant, it was a girl, and her name was Mica. We went out to buy several over-the-counter pregnancy tests, and they all came back the same—positive. We just did not believe it, so we went to the doctor and paid $107 for a blood pregnancy test with the same result, positive. We were elated. She was a vaginal delivery. As my first child, she was remarkably easy, with only a few hours of labor and no epidural or any pain medication of sort. Three pushes, and she was born into the world. She was beautiful from first sight.

My second child is Michael. He is two and a half years younger than his sister. Because I already had a girl, at this point, I prayed for a boy. This child, at some point, had me on bed rest for three weeks leading up to his birth. He was a C-section, emergency delivery, for he was in distress and not moving when we rushed to the hospital. His dad and I were so worried and afraid, but by the grace of God, we made it to the hospital just in time. Because of our conditions, he was housed in a different ward from me, so it would be days before I could see him. But when I did, I was so happy. He was so handsome, and I knew he was meant to be here.

When my son was about five years old, he said to me, "I asked God if you could be my mom." I was moved beyond tears and believed every word. I asked myself, "What five-year-old would say something like that if it was not from God?" I have thanked the Lord every day for my babies and prayed that his blood continues to cover them forever.

My third baby is this book. I call her *Dented Crown*. It has been long and painstaking, for I tried to abort this book several times. But God would not allow me to. I have notebooks and sticky notes, definitions and scriptures everywhere. Although I was writing stuff down, nothing was making sense to me. One day I sat down and looked over my notebooks and my sticky notes. I had to ask God, "What is this?"

God replied to me, "It's an outline of your chapters for your book."

I thought, "What am I supposed to do with that?"

So I put *Dented Crown* on the shelf. At times, it was out of sight, out of mind, but I would think about it often. I would continue to jot down different things when it would come to me in my notebooks or on sticky notes, whatever was nearby. God has a way of getting your attention—moving things out of your way to bring it back to the forefront. You see, I never thought I was good enough to write a book, this book, *Dented Crown*. My third child had a hold on me and would not leave my spirit alone even when I showed no interest. So I decided to finally give birth, bring it to fruition, and in a few months, delivered her. I was pleased with how God filled in the chapters. I prayed that this book does exactly what God intended it for; for you to realize your purpose even if your crown is dented. My crown has fallen off many times, yet it has never broken.

Dented Crown is about the love that God has for you, the power that God has instilled in you, and the joy that is waiting for you once you realize your purpose.

"Come, follow me," Jesus said, "And I will
send you out to fish for people."
—Matthew 4:19 NIV

Chapter 1

Energy
The capacity or power to do work, such as the capacity to move an object (of a given mass) by the application of force. Energy can exist in a variety of forms, such as electrical, mechanical, chemical, thermal, or nuclear, and can be transformed from one to another.

Matter
Material substance that constitutes the observable universe and together with energy, forms the basis of all objective phenomena.

We are all energy and matter. Our actions can have a cause and effect in our lives as well as others. So be careful. What you cause that can affect someone's life—their outcome, their balance, their joy, their peace, their happiness. Your cause and effect can cause ups and downs in someone's life, a disconnect from their mind, body, or soul. You are responsible for your own actions, for God has given us free will, and as a result of that, we need to remain mindful of how we walk through this life so as not to cause or effect anyone harm. It's okay to unplug and reboot, for we are living in a society that's all about the "Right now," the "Hurry up," and the "What's taking so long?" I have noticed that no one has patience anymore. We are in a hurry to go nowhere fast. There are no more *please*s and *thank you*s. I am so grateful that God has never hurried us up; his patience with us is infinite, and his love is agape—the greatest love we will ever know.

We need to slow down and enjoy the life that God has given us. He made us in his image. Take a moment and wrap your head around that.

Energy and matter—the energy you emit from your body is a matter of your character. You can walk into a room and change the whole atmosphere from your energy. It matters how you move. It matters how you think. It matters how you carry yourself. Would God approve? Use your energy and the presence of your matter to uplift someone. You, I, we never know what someone is going through and how a kind word, smile, or gesture can change their mood. Use your energy and matter to inspire and to allow people to see the God in you.

As long as I could remember, I thought I never mattered to people. I was born to a fifteen-year-old mother who was, and at this point, still is using drugs and alcohol. So even from the beginning, my life didn't matter. I was raised by my grandmother, who had children of her own. Six, as a matter of fact—my mother being counted as one. So to add a baby—and then later, two more, my brother and sister—it was quite a burden placed upon my grandmother. My mother ran away from home long before I was born and was never really present in my life after my birth. I always wanted to know why she didn't love me, why there was no father figure present, never knowing if he even knew about me and if he did, why he never did come for me. I have struggled with those questions for years, long into my adulthood.

Please don't mistake what I'm saying. I was very grateful to grow up in a household without drugs or alcohol—one with some structure, where I was able to eat daily, have clean clothes, and able to go to school and have friends as I became an adult. Looking back, I realized I was loved the best way they knew how. But through my childhood, teen ages, and even young adulthood, the mental anguish and the physical abuse that I had to endure was way more than I thought I could handle. My energy and matter did not and could not burn. I was nothing who came from nothing, who was going to be nothing. Imagine feeling like that as a child because someone's energy and matter is way greater than yours and they are not aware of the power it carries, nor are they concerned with that. Imagine not knowing who you are or who you are going to be. Imagine wanting to end your own life even as a child. Imagine questioning God as a child and not believing he's answering you.

I was a child, already in my young life feeling empty and lost, rejected, and dejected. I was told no one wanted me, not my mom or my dad. With that being said to me, I was already behind the eight ball. How could your mom or dad not want you? You're a baby who didn't ask to be here on earth, born into a world like this. As a teenager, I tried to come into myself and be normal like other teenagers—I just wasn't. I had friends in high school, some of whom I would like to think are still friends. I wasn't allowed to hang out and be a teen, one party every now and then. But I worked a full-time job after school every day and weekends. At this point in my life, I had a fire brewing in my belly. Something that was indescribable but also undeniable. Something that kept me in check and grounded when I wanted to be defiant. I knew I had an energy around me, something that protected me from the mental as well as the physical abuse. When I wanted to hang my head down and be "Woe is me!" The fire in my belly would not allow that.

Daily, at this point in my life, it is almost like a tug-of-war with good but never evil. It was more like sadness, more like emptiness, but that fire I carried in my belly wouldn't allow me to veer too far into darkness. One day I was determined to extinguish this fire in my belly, to put it out because it hadn't done me any good. I was lost and in turmoil with my mentality. The harder I tried to figure myself out, the deeper I went into my misery, feeling melancholy daily, unwanted, unloved, and broken. These were my thoughts daily, and at some point, *black* and *ugly* got thrown into the mix. One day after school, I'm not sure what set me off, but all of my ugly daily thoughts were stirred up. At that point, I had no energy. My life didn't matter.

Once I got home from school, I went into the bathroom and proceeded to take a cocktail of pills from the medicine cabinet, a handful. I took the cocktail of pills and went to sleep, unbeknownst to anyone. When I woke up the next day, I originally thought I was dead. Once I cleared my eyes, I realized I wasn't. As tears streamed down my face, I asked the Lord, "Why not?" And the Lord said to me as clear as day, "Not this way. I am your Father, and I am with you always."

Surprisingly, I had no side effects from my failed attempt at ending my life. From that moment on, I began thinking differently and developed a confidence that I never had before. Suddenly all the negative words that have been said to me and plagued me through-out my childhood no longer had a hold on me, no longer affected how I thought. I knew that I was black and beautiful, loved and cared for by a parent. That was the greatest on earth, far better than what I thought I was missing. The fire in my belly was blazing again. It was like I was regenerated, reborn, like scales had been peeled back from my eyes. My energy was present and palpable and my life now matters.

What I did not know at the time is that because of God's grace and mercy, the showing of little ole me favored over my life, my enemy was now aware of my presence, and now I would be in the fight of my life. You see, the enemy wasn't worried about me because he thought he had me. He wasn't even worried about the fact that God loved me. What worried him was my awareness of God's love for me, and I no longer had to feel alone. I have learned that one trick the enemy has is to make you believe you are alone and there is no way out.

He preys on our brokenness, hoping that we would never find our way to God. I say it that way because I know God is and has always been with us. It is we who let his hand go and act as if we are alone. You and I must know he is ever present.

Chapter 2

Faith
Complete trust or confidence in someone
or something.

Good is faithful to us. If God is faithful to us, why can't we be faithful to him and each other? Where is our complete trust in anything? In writing this book, I had to ask myself many of the same questions. So in no way am I looking down on anyone, let's make that clear. I may make reference to *I, you,* and *we* at moments in this book. I am very thankful that God is still working on me.

So back to faith, walk out on it. If God has revealed your purpose or impregnated you with an idea, walk out on it; let go of fear and step into your purpose. Everyone is born with some kind of purpose. You may not know it or even want to know, but it's there. Because we have free will, we change the course of our lives, maybe on purpose or maybe unknowingly. Nevertheless, as a result of free will, we alter who we are and who we may become. Years may go by before we are able to get back on track, if we ever do. By not listening to or hearing the voice of God, we can change the whole game of our life.

Did you hear me say this book has been in my spirit for several years? God never gave up on me, but I never lost my hunger for my purpose. God made us so uniquely. He has given us every power we would need to live our best lives, but we get in our own way and stop the ball from rolling without knowing what we have done. But thank goodness, it's never too late to change the ability to be who we are meant to be. Unlocking that person takes a little time but is never impossible.

The enemy wants you to be paralyzed and makes you believe that it's too late. God says, "I am with you always." ALWAYS. *Always* is the keyword. Faith mustard-seed size, let that sink in.

Have faith. Never be ashamed of falling down. Use it as a stepping-stone, and get up gracefully. Dust yourself off, and use it as a lesson learned. Grow from it, and maybe even laugh about it later. While we may not know who we are, the enemy is aware of our power and will not stop until it is destroyed if we allow it. Shadows of doubt are the works of the enemy. God is not in shadows, nor does he cast doubt. You have to be careful of who you allow in your ear, head, and even in your presence. People will say things to bring you down and put you under; like in my case when I was young. Keep in mind, there are chaos agents in the world. Wrap your thoughts around the will of God, and allow his will to consume you. Allow his will to work. Surrender your will and never be afraid. Fear is not of God. God is always faithful to us (2 Thessalonians 3:3).

After my suicide attempt, I was able to recognize my enemy, and he was able to recognize me. For God had showed me great favor and forgave me for trying to take away the greatest gift he had given me—my life. From that day on, I am a believer that God knows you and your purpose long before your parents ever met. Imagine that, you were handpicked by the Creator.

You won that race and fertilized that egg, to be born to those two people, precisely on that day, precisely at that time. Which brings me to that phase in my life where I had the audacity to question God. Why would he allow me to be born to a mother addicted to drugs and alcohol, with a father five years older than my fifteen-year-old mother whom I have never seen? Why didn't he love me enough to want me? Why am I black and so dark? Why must I go through mental anguish and physical abuse? Why am I broken? Why is my family broken and dysfunctional? Why, why, why? I could go on and on, but you get the gist. Most of these questions plagued me like a curse that had been placed on me most of my childhood. I was young and foolish enough to believe that.

But believe it or not, God would always oblige me with an answer, not necessarily right away but always at the right time. It was not always in the form of hearing his voice. Sometimes he would place people in my life to give me a word or show me something in a dream.

When I first noticed I had the ability to dream—dreams that would come to pass—it scared the life out of me. I thought, in my foolishness, that it was a curse. After a while, I was afraid to dream for fear of what I would see and what's to come. I need to explain a little: the dreams were not dreadful or frightening; I just didn't know how to handle it. If I had to describe them, I would say they were calming and preparing my spirit for what was to come. And I still asked God to remove it. Fear is not of God (Isaiah 43:1 NIV). God said, "I have summoned you by name; you are mine." Please excuse me while I take a praise break—hallelujah! I can only say I wish I knew what I know now. God granted my request, and my dreams stopped. Well, maybe you could guess it. After a while, I missed my dreams. I didn't feel right, and I prayed for the return of them. It didn't happen right away, but God restored my dreams. I'm so grateful for his faithfulness because I was a fool.

I don't think we stop and realize how much grace is afforded to us. At this point in my life, I am old enough to know and do better. After God restored my dreams, I begged him for forgiveness, to not give up on me like I felt my parents did. God said to me, "All you have to do is lift your hand up to me." I have a very vivid imagination, so to me, it was as if a child was holding a parent's hand walking down the street.

What comes back to me is that when God saved me, he once again reminded me that he was my father and he would never leave me. I decided since God was so faithful to someone like me—a nobody, a bastard child—let me be faithful to him. How hard could that be, to walk the walk and talk the talk? Easier said than done. The enemy is right there waiting on you to stumble and fall. Never be afraid to stumble and fall, for we are made in God's image though we are flesh born into sin. Like a stalker, the enemy is lying in wait to do what he does best—steal, kill, and destroy. And to me, that means steal your spirit, kill your joy, and destroy your life. I stopped questioning God about the misery I thought my young life was and started asking God to help me stay focus on his will.

Keep in mind I was still young—late adolescence to early twenties—as I began to walk this walk and talk this talk. I did not realize I wasn't fully equipped to deal with this enemy, for his power was strong. Because my power was getting stronger, maybe you can say I was a part-time Christian and maybe even a little cocky walking a fine line of Christianity. I grew up in and loved going to the church. The church is where I met my first boyfriend. Like the boss I was, I told him he was going to be my boyfriend, and he said okay. We were together for a long time. He was my first in everything—my first love, my prom date, my first fiancé, my first baby daddy, the first man to cheat on me, my first heartache and pain. He didn't ask—of course not—for me to make him my everything, my whole world, but I did. And over time, my focus and the vow I made to God slowly changed as I had wrapped my life into this man.

I subconsciously made him my god. Yes, we were both in the church but we didn't make God the head of our relationship. We were young. I say that again, wanting to use that as an excuse—it's not. So as the years passed, and the problems came, my light was dimly shining. I wasn't ready for the real world and the cruelty of people. Not only did he cheat on me, he made a baby with someone else while we were together. This was a whole different betrayal, and the beginning of a pattern where my next couple of relationships would have the same outcome (I digress). Again, this was the pain that I didn't cause and couldn't understand how. When you are loving and giving your all to someone, how could they hurt you so bad?

So the brick wall had a foundation, and I developed a defense mechanism; my tongue was as sharp as knives, and one look would kill your soul. I became the "queen of clapback." That would keep people off me and protect this leaky heart, and in a cynical way, I was proud of that. Although I never talked back to my grandmother or any elders, when I was displeased with the actions of others, I would just look at them with that stare I had perfected. My stare could pierce a soul. And slowly that vow I made to God—to be faithful to him and live my life like a child of God who was given grace and mercy early on—had slowly slipped away.

I began to be sad again. I wanted to hurt people the way I was hurting, because hurt people hurt other people. I started losing my focus, not caring about anything including myself, and my sense of my father God not being there like he promised me, slowly smothered my fire. Not having faith in anything or anybody, I was allowing the enemy to use me. I noticed that when you're trying to do right and be good, walking that walk and talking that talk, the wrong looks so much better and easier, like there's no care in the world. In all actuality, you become a miserable person and too close to see how bad you really are. I have no doubt that your energy and your matter are negative, and you surround yourself with the same type of negative people. I have to tell you: for me, the feeling of being heavy and weighted down is never a good feeling. I honestly didn't like walking on the dark side. To me it's like gloom and doom, like a continuous black cloud over your head.

After a while, this situation (we're going to call it a situation) didn't sit well with me. My life started with heartache and pain early on, and I didn't want to be in that again due to my own volition. So I did what I do best—called my father God like the prodigal son. I returned to his bosom, and he ignited my fire again without making me feel rejected, dejected, or broken, wrapping me in his loving arms of protection as if I had never left.

Chapter 3

Consciousness
The state of being awake and aware of
one's surroundings.

When your mind, body, and soul are not aligned, it's time to figure out what's wrong. We have a conscience and a subconscious mind. In talking to my therapist—yes, I said *therapist*—I found out that the subconscious mind holds on to things from our childhood or past and protects us from trauma as much as possible. But it can replicate in our mind for years—the fears, negativity, and the trauma we've endured, also known as repressed, restrained, inhibited or oppressed memories. Isn't that something that the subconscious mind has the ability to function separately from the conscious mind, influencing our actions and feelings, all the while the conscious mind is unaware? Did you know our actions are almost exclusively controlled by the subconscious mind? Wow, take a minute and let that sink in.

So journey with me for a minute. I'm in my early to midtwenties and after my break up with my first love, I was so distraught, discombobulated, and in total denial that this was the end of my world as I knew it. Because I had always been a hard worker, I worked a full-time job all four years of high school so I had money saved. I moved from one state to another, running away from my brokenness, which, by the way, is not possible. I didn't know anyone, but being there had to be better than being in the same state as the man that destroyed my whole world. I'm dramatic, but it's true. And this is where my ability to run mentally and physically to escape pain started. I could've been a track star, but that's a whole different topic. Of course, at this time, I knew nothing about conscious and subconscious mind. But I surely was packing that trauma in feeding my subconscious mind with power.

Anyway, I stayed out of state a little less than a year. I soon started to feel better but I never forgot about him and the pain that he caused me, the betrayal nevertheless. I was trying to live my best life. After a while, I realized I still had that empty feeling, for I had no family or friends there. I decided to return to the state where I was born. As karma would have it, my first job back after returning home would be with…you guessed it. I had the pleasure of working with him. It started off awkward, but he apologized and begged for my forgiveness. I accepted his apology. So we tried to reconnect, but my conscious mind was on revanche. I wanted to hurt him as much as he hurt me. Thank goodness, he left the job to pursue another. He wanted to keep in touch, but I had other plans so I led him astray.

I was still angry and vengeful, but I must say that to this day, I regret my actions. If God had not been so forgiving to me for my attempted suicide, where would I be? If God was vengeful for all the wrong that I have done, where would I be? If God had never allowed me to hear his voice and dream my visions, where would I be? I'm saying that to tell you that sometimes we truly have to forgive and not allow our subconscious mind to dictate our actions and reactions, to focus on our conscious mind on what is in front of you and not what is behind you.

It's the past, so let it go. I'm sure I was missing many of blessings for my behavior, but it felt right. My energy and matter were fine to me (a lie). I actually knew I had the ability to change the energy and atmosphere in a room with my presence, but I did not always use it the right way. I was halfway faithful to God. The nerve I had to be halfway faithful to a God who loves me enough to allow me grace and mercy daily! I didn't purposely hurt people, but if you hurt me, I would purposely hurt you back. Now how is that godlike?

My conscious mind made me believe I was doing the right thing, but my subconscious mind acted out on every bad behavior. Yet I still didn't see a problem with that. I would look around and see people doing all types of foolishness. It appeared to me as if they were happy. I was still empty inside. I was still lonely. I was back to asking my *why, why, why* questions. Why couldn't I partake in the foolishness? God clearly answered that question and said, "You have a purpose, and I'm not done with you." So here came my battle with the right and wrong, the conscious mind and subconscious mind— my battle to find my way again, my path, removing my will and allowing God's will. For anyone who thinks this is easy, think again. Imagine thinking, as long as you could remember, you were never good enough, but God chose you. That's a heavy burden to bear. (I thought and felt like that in my infinite wisdom.) So because I was traumatized in the beginning of my life, my subconscious mind was trying to keep me traumatized and a victim.

But because the love of my God, that agape love, was so great and undeniable, I felt I really needed to make a real change and stop playing before it was too late. One of the things I learned in this journey is to know yourself. One of my favorite sayings is "To thy own self be true." At some point, I learned I was hardwired, programmed, which means I started doing things just because I thought it was the thing to do. It was not necessarily the right thing to do but the bare minimum thing to do. I had to learn how to step outside of myself, my body, my mind, and even the world that I'd known. I had to die mentally to be born spiritually. I had to let go of all the programming that took place from birth on. I vowed again to take on the life that God had for me and reprogrammed my thinking. I wanted more than anything to be happy, healthy, and free from the subconscious mind holds that held me down.

Apparently, my subconscious mind was ruling my life, my decisions, and the judgment I had of myself. I was my own worst critic, the reason why my mind, body, and soul were constantly at war, unable to find peace, joy and happiness as I thought it should be. I had to allow my conscious mind to shut down, almost like a reboot.

So I started doing research on how that could be possible. One way I found was meditation, such as mindfulness or focusing the mind on a particular object thought or activity to train attention and awareness. I wanted to be aware of my conscious actions. The second was manifestation. It is an event, action, or object that clearly shows and embodies something. The third was visualizing (forming a mental image of something; imagining). And last but not least, I kept an open prayer line to my God. Not to pat myself on the back, but I became a prayer warrior.

Just a side note, now that you have just awakened your enemy or enemies to your relationship with God, here will come the attacks. Not to worry though, because I found out that if you are serious about your Father's business, he is serious about you. For every attack and setback, God will continue to grant you favor. I also learned that in this process, the enemy moves in cycles. That was the key thing that I learned about the enemy. For example, mine went like this: First, I would have problems with my man. Once I overcame that, in came problems with my job. Once I defeated that, problems with my children. Once we survived that, there were problems with my house. Once that was fixed, problems with my car... You get the gist of what I'm saying.

Despite anything the enemy thinks he can do to bring you down or destroy you, stay focused and faithful!

And then he repeats the same cycle. Pay attention; it's true. The enemy has no new tricks. I also started journaling almost daily. I found it helpful with visualization and manifesting—one practice I would call great for my reprogramming technique. Remember, no battle is ever easy. But it's not your battle; it's the Lord's. God has told me many times, "Be still" (Psalm 46:10 NIV), but I'm a little hard-headed. The key is believing and trusting in God being faithful to him as he is faithful to you. I am grateful that he has never given up on me and in the process, my programming was changing.

My outlook on my life is different. I no longer see my life the way I used to. I have never been so complete, fulfilled, and satisfied. The fire in my belly is blazing bright again. It's a feeling I can't imagine being without at this point in my life. Don't misunderstand me; it takes work daily. Do things on purpose; let your energy and matter be present. Have at least that mustard-seed faith. Thank God for his mercy, and ask that his will be done. Things will fall into place as they should; your steps have already been ordered (Psalm 37:23–24 NIV).

Chapter 4

Obedience
Compliance with an order, request, or law
or submission to another's authority.

God wants us to be obedient to him and his word, like any good parent. Growing up, you had to be obedient to your parents and follow the rules. Otherwise there were consequences, so why not be obedient to God's word? Do we believe there are no consequences? (John 14:23–24 NIV).

Growing up, I was never a disobedient child. I may have had a defiant attitude. Remember, I had a stare that could pierce your soul. Plus, everybody in my household was scary, so I dared not open my mouth in a disobedient way. I would get in trouble even when I did not start it—ask my brother and sister. I was empty on the inside, as far as feelings were concerned, and tough on the outside. I would sometimes take whoopings for them. At times it would be bad because I wouldn't cry—dumb me. My brother would say to me, "Why don't you cry so it would be over?" I had no idea. I guess it was my stubbornness.

Let's talk about the word *submission* in the context of the definition, "obedience." As an adult woman, I thought it was good to be submissive to my man. The problem with that theory is that it was always the wrong man and not my husband. I'm going to use this theory because even after all these years, it's the only one I have. I had no father figure to guide me and show me how it should be done. I have made many mistakes with that one. I almost built that brick wall over my head after my relationship experiences. While I was in it, I didn't realize I was doing the same things, expecting a different outcome. Always blaming the other person and never looking at myself, I had abandonment issues, which stem from the subconscious mind from birth. Imagine that.

God was still right there with me. He would allow me to dream about certain outcomes so the blows would be easier on me. The heartaches wouldn't hurt so bad because I knew. My intuition would be going off the radar when lies were told to my face, and when I would confront these people, I would get the same response from every one of them—"You're crazy." But I wasn't. My God was protecting me, that much I knew. I wanted to be obedient and submissive to these men because I thought that would make them love me more even after knowing they weren't right for me. I just couldn't let them leave first for fear of abandonment.

Never giving any real thought about being obedient and submissive to my father God who truly loved me. This is where my track-star status came in—me, running. I would turn on my heels and get the *hell* out of the relationship before it would cause me too much damage and pain. You see, my subconscious mind was doing its thing, protecting me from trauma, all the while causing me trauma by replicating my actions and replicating the type of men I wanted. God would always tell me to "be still." Here comes that great free will I have, wanting to believe the next one will be the right one—nope!

So just recently, I decided to be obedient to God's word and be still when it comes to me picking a husband. Even the phrase is wrong because the Bible says, "He who finds a wife finds what is good" (Proverbs 18:22 NIV). To be honest, one of my biggest problems and fears (fear is not of God) with my husband-finding more recently is my age, the time, and perhaps, a generational curse. My age because I am a woman at a certain age, and we all know beauty can fade. I look in the mirror daily and see a new wrinkle, but I am still beautiful to me. Time because there are more years behind me than in front of me. Last but not least, a generational curse because my mother has never been married. Is that my fate as well? I know that I was looking for that love from men that I didn't receive as a child but had it all along in God, who has NEVER hurt me or forsaken me. So for me, whatever God's will is my will. In the meantime, I will continue to be obedient to his word and continue to let that fire burn blazing bright in my belly. I am learning to love myself more and more as he loves me, for I am worthy. My crown may be a little dented, but I am a child of the King, no less!

Chapter 5

Discernment
The ability to obtain sharp perceptions.

S pritually check the backgrounds of people coming into your life. Pray for the spirit of discernment. It could save you from wasting your time and energy on people who really don't belong in your life, from people that could possible do you harm mentally, spiritually, physically, and emotionally. I always felt like I had insight on people and things but didn't know what it really meant and what to do with it, like a puzzle piece that was always put in the wrong place. I now know that God has blessed me with so many gifts, and it has taken me this long to really want to know and understand the beauty in it. I am like a caterpillar trying to become a butterfly; it is a process. But imagine when the process is completed. She is so beautiful and looks nothing like when first she started.

I rejoiced in his wonder. So I started to pray for clarity and understanding to get to the bottom of the awkwardness. Just like with my dreams, I didn't know what it all meant. I didn't know how to embrace the beauty, that fire that never burned out. In hindsight I'm grateful that it never did, that he—my God and my Father—never left me and didn't let me die all those years ago because he knew my purpose and my wealth even when I was too ignorant I didn't know. I was like that caterpillar crawling on the ground that would soon have colorful beautiful wings, able to fly high and impress the world just by being a butterfly.

I began to pray and pray. God continued to strengthen my insight. My spirit of discernment kicked into gear (1 Corinthians

2:14–16 NIV). I was drawn to like-minded people, spiritual people, and people with a purpose. For the pretenders, I see you. The enemy is a great pretender, but when you have the spirit of discernment, there is no hiding. Just the near presence of the enemy can irritate your soul but not get it twisted. Your presence irritates him as well.

So I was working a job I loved, and I thought I would retire from it. Keep in mind that the enemy is ever present and lurking in the shadows. The person who was an assistant to the boss was over my department and as luck—I don't believe in luck—would have it, she was an agent of the enemy. I was able to "see" her from the beginning. The enemy doesn't like to be seen. This place was brand-new as far as this venture of the company goes. We were about twelve employees under her leadership. She found a way to run ten away. They quit within six months. I wasn't going to quit. I loved it there. It was close to home. The opportunity for growth outside her negative energy and matter and the environment was good. Well, long story short, she found a way to get me fired. I've been in my career for twenty-seven years, and I've never been fired. Twenty-seven years. Like I told y'all, I was a woman of a certain age.

Back in the day, I would have been devastated, but glory to God, I wasn't. I was kind of disappointed because of the attack on my character. But only on paper because the people that know me, they know me. They know my character. They know I will always fight for the underdog, that I am on the side of right and not wrong not under any circumstances. When you have the spirit of discernment, the enemy will try to attack your integrity and your character. The Bible says, "No weapons formed against me shall prosper" (Isaiah 54:17 NIV).

Anyway, remember how I talked about being impregnated with a book? After several years of taking notes and writing down ideas, God said to me, "Now is the time, so now is the time." God has always been faithful to me, so why not be obedient to him? God said his word would never come back void. Within a few weeks of being fired, I started to write my baby—this book. I didn't even stop to feel sorry for myself or worry about how I was going to pay my bills and mortgage buy food, etc. For the first time in my life, I was totally at peace with my purpose. What could have been an obstacle turned out to be a blessing. This time off has given me the opportunity to write my book. This may have just been a dream that would have never come to fruition. God has a way of turning things.

Chapter 6

Meditation
A practice where an individual uses a technique-such as mindfulness, or focusing on the mine on a particular object, thought or activity to train attention and awareness and achieve a mentally clear and emotionally calm and stable state.

Joshua 1:8 NIV

I learned to meditate daily even if it was only for a few moments. I started slow, and as time went on, I increased my time, even falling asleep while doing it. I would set aside a quiet time on purpose, purposely focusing on God's will for me. I learned to relax my mind as well as my body. Sometimes I would use background music or noise like the sound of rain. I particularly liked the rain with thunder. I would go on to discover burning oils and incense. It helped me to be in a more relaxed state. The good-smelling scents enhanced my experience. In the process of doing this, I started to believe I was changing my subconscious mind, therefore allowing my conscious mind to be aware, focus less on my past trauma, rewrite my script and change the ending, accept my blessings without feeling like I wasn't worthy of God's love, his promises, and his gifts that he promised me and only me.

I know that what God has for me is for me, and NOBODY can change that. So now at this point, I am a meditating, journaling, visualizing, and manifesting prayer warrior with a dented crown whom God saw worthy of his love. For that, I must say HALLELUJAH anyhow! You, I, we must trust God and trust the process. God said he would never forsake us. He is only asking that we have faith the size of a small mustard seed. Every time I think about that, it just blows my mind.

Conclusion

This was and is still my journey, I pray your journey is smooth. Every move you make is ordered by God. I pray this book helps someone who may just need to know that you are not alone.

I purposefully left out some details because this wasn't really about me but about how I found my way to God who had never left me, about how God allowed me to find my way to him and what I mentally went through to get there. It's about how God loved me so, and if he could love me so much, imagine how much he loves you!

about the author

The author, Michelle R. Bostic, is on a journey to find her way in this life. God has proven time after time to be there for her, and now she is accepting her place in his heart. She is on a campaign for everyone to find their place in God's heart as well.

Printed in the USA
CPSIA information can be obtained
at www.ICGtesting.com
LVHW050416190823
755495LV00003B/446